IMAGES
of America

DuPont Theatre

IMAGES
of America
DuPont Theatre

Joanna L. Arat

ARCADIA
PUBLISHING

Published by Arcadia Publishing
Charleston, South Carolina

Printed in the United States of America

Library of Congress Control Number: 2012932109

For all general information, please contact Arcadia Publishing:
Telephone 843-853-2070
Fax 843-853-0044
E-mail sales@arcadiapublishing.com
For customer service and orders:
Toll-Free 1-888-313-2665

Visit us on the Internet at www.arcadiapublishing.com

*Dedicated to the employees and patrons, past
and present, of the DuPont Theatre.
You are the true stars of the show.*

CONTENTS

ACKNOWLEDGMENTS

First and foremost, I express my gratitude to the staff members, past and present, at the DuPont Theatre, who were so kind to share their stories and photographs with me. I also appreciate the continued support of my fellow hospitality-marketing colleagues Adam Cofield and Regina Widdoes, as well as my supervisor, marketing and public relations manager Carolyn Grubb, who mentored me through the process. Furthermore, this book would not have been possible without the staff of Hagley Museum and Library, including Lucas Clawson, Judy Stevenson, and Elizabeth Fite. I'm grateful for the assistance provided by Ellen Rendle from the Delaware Historical Society as well as Dennis Steele and his staff from Visual Arts Studio, including Jeff Lukowski and Kay Gilligan. In addition, it was a privilege to speak with Sean Reilly, Marge McNinch, and especially Kathleen Lynch, granddaughter of DuPont Theatre contractor John A. Bader. Special thanks also to DuPont hospitality director Lisa Bolten and DuPont Theatre general manager Annmarie O'Hara-Townsend for their enthusiasm and support of the project. Last but not least, I am extremely grateful for the detailed eye and constructive coaching from my editor, Janet Dill.

When the theater changed its name in 2003, it added a service mark, DuPont[SM] Theatre, denoting its relationship to the company brand. The content of this book, especially anecdotal information, is based on stories people have told me, notes and programs, interviews, and historical memorabilia. Unless the image is otherwise identified, the photographs used in this book appear courtesy of the DuPont Theatre (DT) and Hagley Museum and Library (HML).

INTRODUCTION

The year was 1913. Woodrow Wilson was president, and the specter of global war loomed. DuPont was transforming itself from an explosives manufacturer into an international chemical company with modern, downtown office buildings. In New York, Broadway theaters were earning rave reviews as the "entertainment capital of America." This phenomenon led three DuPont executives who shared a dream to build a theater in Wilmington, Delaware, that would showcase "the finest entertainment possible" as well as providing the community with a venue for nonprofit events, lectures, and business meetings. DuPont treasurer John J. Raskob joined Pierre S. du Pont and R.R.M. Carpenter in turning this dream into a reality. Their intent was to build a theater large enough to accommodate any New York show as a "dress rehearsal venue" while enhancing the quality of life for DuPont employees and Wilmington residents.

It was clear that the theater's location would be key to its success. The partners decided to build in a courtyard on Market Street between Tenth and Eleventh Streets, known as Pinkett's Court at the time. It was no coincidence that the site they chose adjoined the footprint of the elegant new Hotel du Pont, which had just celebrated its grand opening on January 15, 1913.

Well-known New York architect Charles A. Rich was commissioned to design a theater closely resembling the Playhouse in New York. The Wilmington firm of Brown and Whiteside assisted. On April 3, 1913, J.A. Bader & Co. clinched the construction contract with a low bid of $122,960. Two weeks later, on April 15, construction commenced.

A 100-man crew worked for 150 consecutive days to construct the theater that would be called the Playhouse. It was one of the largest theaters of its time. Measuring 38 feet deep and 85 feet wide, the stage could easily accommodate almost any traveling show. On opening night, October 15, 1913, crowds and press gathered for the spectacle. Never before had there been a theater located within such an elegant hotel, and the idea of offering fine dining, overnight accommodations, and a Broadway show was unique. The first production to grace the new stage was *Bought and Paid For*. Ticket prices started at 25¢ for gallery seating.

William A. Brady, a New York producer, leased the theater for the first five years. He was best known for thrilling audiences with stage effects that included an action-packed train wreck, an automobile accident, and a foxhunt—with live animals on stage—during his production of *The Whip*. Subsequent lessees continued presenting creative stage shows but diversified and broadened theater offerings by introducing ballets, lectures, and even motion pictures. However, despite its early success, the Playhouse struggled to remain profitable as the Great Depression and a citywide flu epidemic dealt blows to ticket sales. Finally, the Shubert brothers, who held the lease in 1928, threatened to shutter the venue. This devastating news prompted the Wilmington Chamber of Commerce to issue a direct appeal for community support. Within a few days, more than 300 subscriptions were sold, ensuring the theater's viability. The Shuberts agreed to continue operating the Playhouse until 1930, when Raymond N. Harris assumed the role during the most challenging seasons of its history. DuPont assumed full management in 1946.

With the rise of the Hollywood silver screen and the conversion of many live theaters into movie houses, the possibility lingered that the show would not go on. However, the Playhouse never converted, thus earning its reputation as the longest continuously operating legitimate theater in the nation. DuPont faced a new challenge in 1949 by undertaking the theater's first major renovation since its opening. The company also introduced more creative marketing strategies, such as affordable student ticket prices, free parking for theatergoers, a telephone reservation system, and new dinner-theater promotions. A later improvement involved installing an infrared sound system to improve sound quality for the hearing impaired. The combined effort during these 35 years helped increase the number of subscriptions from 400 to more than 4,000.

By the late 1980s, the Playhouse prepared to celebrate its 75th anniversary, having earned the moniker "Wilmington's Little Broadway." A star-filled season, lobby renovations, and even a subscribers' sweepstakes for a trip to London helped create a buzz. Shows were running for longer spans, and subscriber counts were growing. The introduction of a computerized ticketing system in the box office simplified the reservation process. In 1988, the Children's Series began bringing thousands of elementary students to learn about a variety of topics, such as science, history, literature, and art, through the magic of live theater at an affordable price. This program now reaches more than 40,000 children per year. Improvements continued in the 1990s with updated stage rigging, wheelchair access, a life-safety program, and a sky mural painted on the ceiling.

With the new millennium came new ebbs and flows for the Playhouse. The tragic events of September 11, 2001, created a cloud of sadness that descended on theatergoers, both in the New York City Theater District and for the patrons of the Playhouse. While New York City's Broadway went dark for two days, the opening of the Playhouse's 89th season was just days away. Fortunately, subscribers continued to purchase seats, seeking comfort in entertainment, and the Playhouse remained open. In February 2003, the Playhouse name changed to the DuPont℠ Theatre. Uniting with its sister properties, the Hotel du Pont and the DuPont Country Club, all three properties joined under the umbrella of DuPont Hospitality.

Through trials and triumphs, the DuPont Theatre stands proud of maintaining its status as the oldest legitimate continually operating theater in the country. As recent winner of the *Wilmington News Journal* Reader's Choice award for "Best Live Arts Venue" in 2011, the DuPont Theatre has entertained audiences for 100 seasons of fantastic Broadway shows, such as *Cat on a Hot Tin Roof*, *Grease*, *Mama Mia*, *Cats*, and *Les Miserables*. The stage has proudly welcomed stars such as Lucille Ball, Orson Wells, Helen Hayes, Bette Davis, Fred Astaire, Louis Armstrong, Christopher Plummer, Tommy Tune, Julie Andrews, and more.

One

SETTING THE STAGE
CONSTRUCTION OF THE PLAYHOUSE IN THE EXPANDING CITY OF WILMINGTON

MARKET STREET, 1905. This photograph, taken on December 12, 1905, shows the location where the DuPont Building would be constructed just over a year later in 1907. The local YMCA, four-story Harkness Building, and William S. Watt's home and store had occupied the land. (Courtesy of HML.)

SKETCH OF DUPONT BUILDING.
This early-20th-century sketch
shows the DuPont Building
where it would be located at
Tenth and Market Streets
in downtown Wilmington.
The Playhouse was the third
of six sections to be added
to the building, starting in
December 1905 and completed
in 1931. (Courtesy of Delaware
Historical Society.)

DUPONT BUILDING. As DuPont
business transitioned from gunpowder
and other explosives in factories and
mills to an international chemical
company, executive office suites
became more essential. A modern
office building, erected in 1907 in the
center of downtown Wilmington, has
served as headquarters for executives,
researchers, branch managers, and
DuPont regional and international
customers. (Courtesy of HML.)

HOTEL DU PONT. It took more than two years for Italian and French craftsmen to construct the luxurious Hotel du Pont in the DuPont Building. The plans were to erect a hotel so grand that it would compliment the international prestige of the company itself and parallel world-renowned hotels in Europe. The Hotel du Pont was opened on January 15, 1913, offering first-class accommodations and fine dining to community members and their guests. Originally built with 150 guest rooms, the hotel nearly doubled its size in 1918 with the addition of 118 more guest rooms, a newly relocated lobby, and the grand Gold Ballroom. (Both, courtesy of HML.)

JOHN J. RASKOB. John J. Raskob, treasurer of DuPont, sparked the initial concept of building a theater in Wilmington. His dream, shared with DuPont executive R.R.M. Carpenter, was to construct the theater adjacent to the Hotel du Pont, combining world-class dining and lodging with Broadway entertainment. Raskob's background in financial management helped persuade DuPont president Pierre S. du Pont to approve and fund this business venture. (Courtesy of HML.)

PIERRE S. DU PONT. Pierre S. du Pont resided in an apartment at the adjacent Hotel du Pont. His love of music and theater productions made him a frequent patron of the Playhouse on opening nights. However, he preferred not to be in the public eye, so he immediately retreated to his apartment after each show. (Courtesy of HML.)

FORM 4472.Y.

WILMINGTON TRUST BUILDING CORPORATION,

(WILMINGTON, DELAWARE.

7

March 10th, 1913.

James P. Winchester, President,
        Wilmington Trust Company,
              B u i l d i n g.

Dear Mr. Winchester,

In reference to the matter of theatre bonds, about
which we talked this morning, I beg to advise as follows:-

It is my plan to erect a theatre on land immediately
to the rear of the Du Pont Building, the total value of which will
be between $170 000 and $180 000. To finance this it is proposed
to organize a new company, say The Playhouse Company, under the
laws of Delaware, which company will issue $110 000, 5%, twenty-
five year Sinking Fund gold bonds. The company will own the
theatre property, and it is proposed that the bonds - represent-
ing less than two-thirds of the value of the property - shall
be an absolute first mortgage and be guaranteed principal and
interest by the Du Pont Building Corporation, which latter corporation will give the PlayHouse Company right of ingress and
egress for pedestrian traffic through the Du Pont Building.
The plot of land on which it is proposed to build the theatre
is 120' x 120' and we have conservatively appraised its value
at $4.00 per square foot.

It is proposed that The Playhouse Company lease this
theatre to William A. Brady of New York, who is willing to take
it for a period of at least ten years at a rental of $11 000 per
annum (which is twice the bond interest). The writer, however,

DuPont Interest Letter. John J. Raskob presented this letter to the president of Wilmington Trust Bank on March 10, 1913, outlining his financial business plans for building a theater in Pinkett's Court. He further described how it would serve as a business venture, present the finest entertainment, and provide community meeting space for rallies, charitable events, and town meetings. He also disclosed the identity of the first theater lessee, William A. Brady. (Courtesy of HML.)

CONTRACTOR J.A. BADER & CO. J.A. Bader & Co., incorporated in 1910, was operated by New York native John A. Bader. Bader, bidding against eight competitors, captured the Playhouse project with his bid of $122,960. The company's final project was building the Wilmington all-boys high school, Salesianum, in 1957. (Courtesy of Kathleen Lynch.)

MERWIN O. BADER. Merwin O. Bader joined his father's business when he was only 18 years old. For his first project, he helped his father construct the Playhouse. His daughter Kathleen Lynch recalls her father's passion for architecture, as well as the hobby he developed in the late 1940s. A gifted storyteller, Bader grew to love the theater and became a principal actor at the Wilmington Drama League. (Courtesy of Kathleen Lynch.)

BREAKING GROUND. While the original contract stipulated a construction start date of April 1, 1913, ground was not actually broken until April 23, 1913, because sheds were located on the designated site. Two-horse and six-horse teams worked to clear the debris, a task quite difficult due to rains creating a heavy clay mud. From start to finish, it took the strength and dedication of 100 men over 150 working days to complete the project in time for opening night on October 15, 1913. (Courtesy of DT.)

STRUCTURAL MATERIALS. The construction of the theater required an impressive 750,000 bricks, 2,000 barrels of cement, 27,000 cubic feet of concrete weighing 2,000 tons, 1,400 tons of stone, 500 tons of plaster, 1,800 tons of sand, and 125,000 feet of lumber. Most of the lumber was used for scaffolding and the stage. (Both, courtesy of DT.)

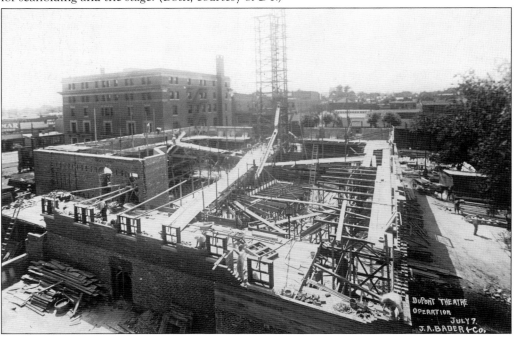

UNOBSTRUCTED VIEWS. A noteworthy feature in the design and construction of the theater was the absence of columns to support the gallery. Thus, all 1,223 seats had an unobstructed view of the stage. The architect accomplished this with counterbalancing structural cantilevers built into the walls along the back of the theater to support the gallery and balcony. (Courtesy of DT.)

THE PLAYHOUSE STAGE. The size of the stage was the most impressive feature of the Playhouse. Measuring 38 feet deep and 85 feet wide, it exceeded the stage dimensions of nearly every theater in New York, including the Manhattan Opera House. Such a grand scale made the Playhouse a "dress rehearsal venue," accommodating theatrical productions from larger metropolitan cities. (Courtesy of HML.)

CONCRETE CANTILE[VE]RS [+]POSTS UNDER. BALCONY
DUPONT THEATR[E]
J.A.BADER +Co.

DUPONT THEATRE
OPERATION JUNE 30

REINFORCED CONCRETE. One of the greatest obstacles encountered during construction was in May 1913, when contractor John A. Bader learned that the structural steel that was required to support the roof and balcony could not be obtained for the project. He would have to use reinforced concrete instead. Famous for his work in reinforced concrete design, Layton F. Smith of Baltimore, Maryland, redesigned the structural support. (Courtesy of DT.)

TWO-MONTH PROGRESS. By June 1913, all foundations had been laid, with the back wall of the theater built up 20 feet tall. Residents were impressed that the auditorium had no basement below, which prevented collapsing. Instead, basements were built under lobbies and the stage. Others were shocked that with such a large stage, the small auditorium was only expected to seat 1,300. (Courtesy of DT.)

18

FIREPROOF STRUCTURE. The Playhouse received praise for the outstanding safety measures incorporated in its design and construction. Built almost entirely of brick and concrete, the theater was completely fireproof. Three main entrances and 11 fire exits equipped with pressure bolts added to fire precautions. The finished theater only contained a small amount of lumber for the stage floor. (Courtesy of DT.)

THE STEEL GIRDER. A theater of this size required a completely fireproofed steel girder that weighed 120 tons to support the main roof. Not only was this the largest girder ever used in any theater, it was also the third largest in the world. To ensure compliance with safety regulations, engineers tested the strength of the girder 30 days after installation and were praised when it withstood the weight of 120,000 pounds of cement. (Courtesy of DT.)

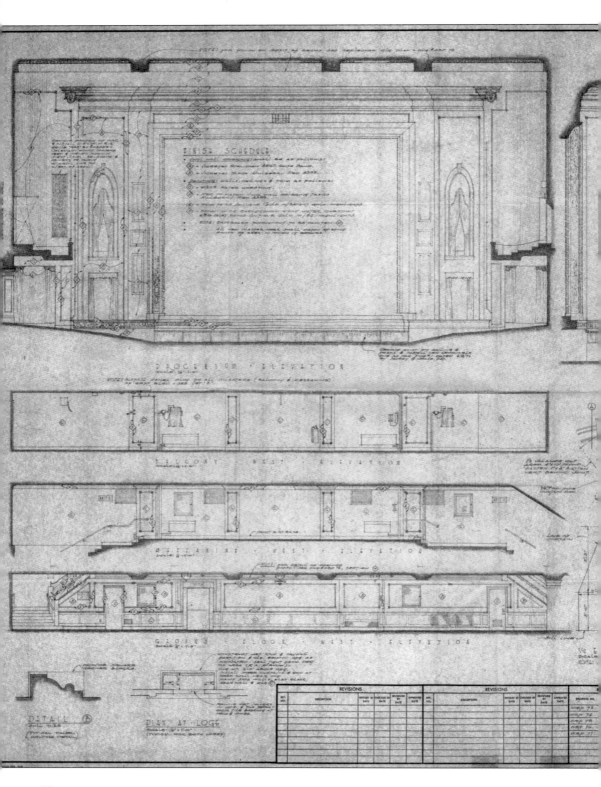

PROCENIUM · ELEVATION

BALCONY WEST · ELEVATION

MEZZANINE · WEST · ELEVATION

LADIES · FLOOR · WEST · ELEVATION

DETAIL

PLAN · AT · LOGE

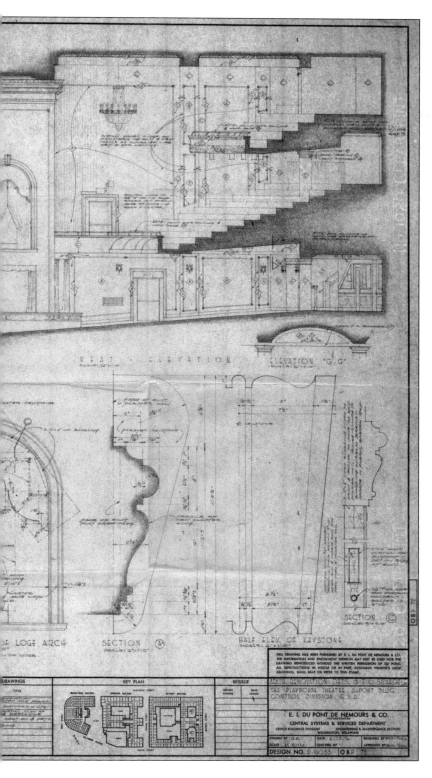

PAINTING THE THEATER. This blueprint of the theater includes the finish schedule for designated paint colors used in the interior. Wall coverings were painted in white sand and Tasco mulberry red. Walls, ceilings, and trim moldings were painted in water chestnut, Tasco mulberry red, and antique gold. (Courtesy of HML.)

PLAYHOUSE DECORATOR. All construction ceased for days while the 85-foot concrete girder hardened for fear that any vibration would damage it. To make up for lost time and still meet the unmovable opening night deadline, decorator William Eckhart began painting while plaster was drying, using special considerations for fading paint and toning while he created the masterpiece of rich gold and maroon ceilings, walls, and columns. (Courtesy of DT.)

BALCONY STEPS. Another major delay during the construction of the theater nearly prevented the grand opening on its designated date. It was discovered that the intended building material of cast iron stone was no longer available to build the balcony steps. John A. Bader quickly decided to substitute artificial Caen stone instead, and the balcony steps were completed with two days to spare. (Courtesy of DT.)

SPACIOUS SEATING. Space and comfort were not compromised in the selection of theater seats. The selected chairs were 22 inches wide, which was approximately four inches wider than the average theater seat. The 10-tiered balcony was more spacious than any New York City theater; it allowed three feet between each of the tiers. (Courtesy of HML.)

MULTIPLE THEATER ENTRANCES. Recognized as one of the safest and most comfortable theaters in the country, the Playhouse offered the convenience of three street entrances. Patrons could enter the building from the front door of the Hotel du Pont on Eleventh Street, the main Playhouse entrance on Market Street, or an additional entrance on Tenth Street, facilitating transportation options before and after each show. (Courtesy of DT.)

SUBCONTRACTORS. Contractors and Wilmington passersby doubted that construction would be completed within the dates of the building contract, especially because head contractor John A. Bader signed the contract 16 days after the intended start date. Bader credited the work of subcontractors who were able to meet deadlines and shift to new roles as needed. (Courtesy of DT.)

MARKET STREET POSTCARD. This postcard reproduction shows an evening on Market Street around 1940. The view from Eleventh Street looks south toward the Wilmington riverfront. During construction, the property was referred to as the DuPont Theatre. In September 1913, just prior to the opening of the theater, a vertical electric sign lit up to reveal the name "Playhouse." (Courtesy of Delaware Historical Society.)

Two

ON WITH THE SHOW
STORIES, STARS, AND SHOWS
FROM 1913 TO 1986

OPENING NIGHT. On October 15, 1913, DuPont employee A.C. Bonnell purchased the first Playhouse ticket at 9:40 a.m. By evening, formally dressed theater patrons were met by press flashbulbs for the first performance. The first lessee, William A. Brady, greeted enthusiastic crowds by outlining his policy to bring the best productions to the Playhouse. Wilmington mayor Harrison Howell presented contractor John A. Bader with two gifts: a gold watch from DuPont executives for completing the Playhouse two days early and a watch chain from his subcontractors and employees for being so courteous. The opening show, *Bought and Paid For*, was not nearly as admired as the luxurious theater itself. Local papers declared the Playhouse "the final accessory" in the city of Wilmington. (Courtesy of HML.)

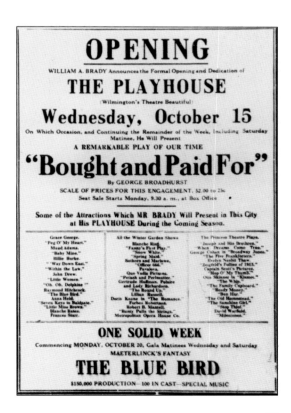

AUSPICIOUS OPENING. The daily newspaper, the *Wilmington Morning News*, praised the new theater in an article called "Auspicious Opening of the New Playhouse," published on October 16, 1913. The article proclaimed that the addition of this new theater "meant that at last, Wilmington should be as other cities—that it should have the best in the way of metropolitan dramas and companies. . . . It meant the opening of a house which completed the list of entertainments to which Wilmington is entitled." (Courtesy of DT.)

DISTINGUISHED GUESTS. On opening night, the house was full. The first lessee, William A. Brady, was proud to fill box seats with political figures like Gov. Charles R. Miller and Mayor Harrison Howell. A common misconception about box seats is that they provide the best view in the house. On the contrary, these private boxes, located on the left and right wings of the theater above orchestra level, have a limited view of the entire stage; however, it's not about seeing in the box seats, it is about being seen. Governor Miller congratulated the city of Wilmington for a venue that he predicted would receive praise equal to that of the newly opened Hotel du Pont. (Courtesy of HML.)

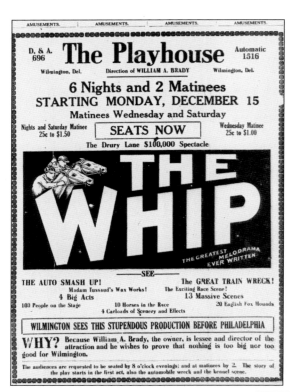

THE WHIP POSTER. The Playhouse performance of *The Whip* on December 15, 1913, astounded audiences with a live automobile accident in the first act. The English drama was also the first performance on a Wilmington stage to feature live animals (horses and hounds) and a railroad wreck in the third act. *Every Evening*, a Wilmington newspaper, raved, "To say that it is realistic and exciting is putting it mildly." (Courtesy of HML.)

ALICE BRADY. The daughter of first Wilmington Playhouse lessee William A. Brady, Alice Brady was no stranger to the theater. Born in 1892, she pursued acting against her father's wishes. She attended opening night at the Playhouse on October 15, 1913, and would later perform on the Playhouse stage in a leading role with a theater group called the Brady Players. She was appropriately nicknamed "Queen of Movie Stars." (Courtesy of DT.)

MARKET STREET, NORTH FROM 8TH STREET, WILMINGTON, DEL.

GOLDEY COLLEGE. Founded by H.S. Goldey in 1886, Goldey College was originally located at Eighth and Market Streets. During the opening season of the Playhouse, Goldey College hosted its 27th commencement for 129 graduates in November 1913. This graduation ceremony was the first non–performing arts event to take place at the Playhouse. (Courtesy of Delaware Historical Society.)

MARKET STREET FROM 9TH STREET, WILMINGTON, DEL.

MARKET STREET BUSINESSES. This postcard depicts the view of Ninth and Market Streets facing north toward the DuPont Building. In the distance on the left is the lighted Playhouse marquee. One prominent downtown Wilmington bank, Equitable Trust, is also on the left. The "for rent" sign on the right indicates that the city was still expanding. (Courtesy of Delaware Historical Society.)

MERRY WHIRL. This photograph, taken in 1915, shows the cast of *Merry Whirl*, a production staged at the Playhouse. The local Wilmington actors and actresses are, from left to right, (sitting) Henryette L. Stadelman, Mary Bringhurst, Mrs. George A. Elliott, Mrs. Philip Marquand, and unidentified; (standing) Mrs. Gamble Latrobe, Edward Bringhurst, John B. Bird, Col. G.A. Elliott, Gamble Latrobe, George Capelle Jr., Peter Wright, and unidentified. (Courtesy of Delaware Historical Society.)

WILMINGTON COURTHOUSE. The original county courthouse, shown in 1916, stood on Market Street between Tenth and Eleventh Streets. The front of the building directly faced the Market Street entrance of the Playhouse. The photograph below shows the courthouse from Eleventh Street with the DuPont Building on the right. The building is in early stages of demolition as the city prepares to develop Rodney Square in 1919. (Both, courtesy of DT.)

A Flu Epidemic. This postcard depicts businesses located on West Tenth Street, including a local shoe repair shop, the Wilmington Automobile Company, and the DuPont Building. At this time, the Playhouse faced its first crisis. A flu epidemic crippled Wilmington in 1918. Some 10,000 cases were reported, prompting the Delaware State Board of Health to close all public buildings and businesses for almost one month. (Courtesy of Delaware Historical Society.)

Earle G. Finney. After purchasing the Playhouse from the Majestic Theatre Company in 1921, Earle G. Finney served as the only manager and owner in DuPont Theatre history. Unfortunately, his lease was doomed on the night of December 11, 1925, during the opening performance of *Song of the Flame.* Just 20 minutes into the performance, the scenery collapsed, walls crumbled, and actors were injured before the curtain lowered. (Courtesy of HML.)

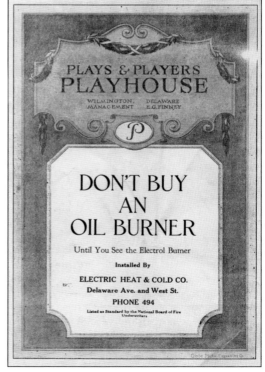

PLAYS & PLAYERS
PLAYHOUSE
WILMINGTON, DELAWARE
MANAGEMENT E.G. FINNEY

P

DON'T BUY
AN
OIL BURNER

Until You See the Electrol Burner

Installed By

ELECTRIC HEAT & COLD CO.
Delaware Ave. and West St.
PHONE 494

Listed as Standard by the National Board of Fire Underwriters

THE SHUBERT PLAYHOUSE. The first name change of the Playhouse occurred in October 1926, when the famous Shubert brothers leased the theater with the "intention to place Wilmington on a metropolitan basis." In an effort to attract more patrons when ticket sales began to decline, they changed the name to the Shubert Playhouse, trying to add the prestige of a New York City theater. (Courtesy of HML.)

Shubert
PLAYHOUSE
Du Pont Building   Wilmington, Del.
SHUBERT THEATRE CORP. LESSEE
Direction LEE *and* J. J. SHUBERT

S-P

Season 1927 - 1928

Press of CANN BROTHERS & KINDIG, Inc., *Wilmington, Del.*

FUNNY FACE. Brother and sister duo Fred and Adele Astaire starred in the George Gershwin Broadway musical *Funny Face* at the Playhouse in November 1927. In 1957, Paramount studios created a film version of the musical with original star Fred Astaire and new up and coming star Audrey Hepburn. (Courtesy of HML.)

33

THE **1930s.** The Great Depression caused a precipitous drop in theater attendance, challenging Raymond N. Harris, then Playhouse manager. He countered by staging shows like the spirited Pulitzer Prize–winning satiric musical *Of Thee I Sing*, by George and Ira Gershwin. Both World War II and the meteoric rise of movies also contributed to his troubles. Harris booked big names including Orson Welles and Helen Hayes before retiring in 1946, when DuPont officially assumed management of the Playhouse. The 1950s brought Broadway sensations and more big stars to Wilmington, among them Shirley Booth, who led the cast of *The Time of the Cuckoo*. (Both, courtesy of HML.)

ELSA LANCHESTER. Before she achieved Hollywood stardom for her leading role in *Bride of Frankenstein* in 1935, Elsa Lanchester and her husband, Charles Laughton, starred in the US premier of *Payment Deferred* at the Playhouse in September 1931. Lanchester returned to the Playhouse in 1952 for the comedy show *Private Music Hall*. (Courtesy of DT.)

THE BARRYMORES. Siblings Ethel, Lionel, and John Barrymore (pictured) dominated the Broadway stage, earning the theater nickname "Royal Family." Each made several appearances on the Playhouse stage in the 1920s and 1930s. In 1996, the Broadway production *Barrymore*, which dramatized the story of John Barrymore's final months, came to the Playhouse stage. Tony Award–winner Christopher Plummer memorably portrayed Barrymore. (Courtesy of DT.)

FORT MILES PLAYERS. This cast photograph portrays the Fort Miles Players on August 31, 1942. The group produced and starred in the musical review *Here We Go,* which toured Fort DuPont and the Playhouse in Wilmington. (Courtesy of Delaware Historical Society.)

CAVALCADE OF AMERICA. This group portrait of the *Cavalcade of America* was taken by Carl W. Thompson on the Playhouse stage around 1950. Pictured here are the chorus, director, announcer, and the pianists who performed in the *Cavalcade of America,* a DuPont-sponsored dramatic radio-turned-television show. It presented highlights and events of interest in American history. The company tagline, as seen here, was "Better things for better living through chemistry." (Courtesy of Delaware Historical Society.)

FREE PARKING

THEATRE SUBSCRIBER
PARKING - HOTEL CAR PARK - 12th & Orange Streets
or when directed
WILMINGTON PARKING AUTHORITY - 13th & Orange Streets
Valid only on theatre ticket date
Evenings 6:00 P.M. to Midnight - Saturday Matinee Noon to 6:00 P.M.

Courtesy of

THE Playhouse THEATRE

POSTWAR PROSPERITY. Playhouse subscriptions flourished under the management of DuPont employee William H. Doerflinger, who served from 1952 until 1986. In his 34 years, he booked Broadway showstoppers, such as *South Pacific* and *Sugar Babies*, and featured big names, such as Bette Davis, Mickey Rooney, and Robert Redford. New marketing incentives also helped boost ticket sales and increase subscribers. Student ticket pricing and new miniseries subscriptions were some of the innovations. Pre-theater dining and a show were bundled together in affordable theater packages. Free parking was also offered to theater subscribers. His aggressive efforts paid off as he increased subscriptions from 400 to more than 2,000 in his first season. (Both, courtesy of HML.)

RODNEY SQUARE. This photograph depicts Rodney Square, located directly across from the DuPont Building's Market Street entrance into the Playhouse around 1950. This space was originally occupied by the county courthouse, which was demolished in 1919. The square is dedicated to Caesar Rodney and has been a popular location for community events such as farmers markets, jazz and blues festivals, and caroling during the holidays. (Courtesy of DT.)

WILMINGTON ON THE ROCKS

Production Created by Jerome H. Cargill Co., Inc.
140 Fifth Avenue, New York, N.Y.

Produced and Directed by Howard Miller

John H. Haas Jr., Musical Director

Make-up by Max Factor

Courtesy of Strawbridge & Clothier

MARCH 12TH AND 13TH, 1965
THE PLAYHOUSE

WILMINGTON ON THE ROCKS. In 1965, the Junior League of Wilmington, a nonprofit women's service group that is committed to volunteerism in the community, hosted a special production at the Playhouse called *Wilmington on the Rocks.* This musical paid tribute to famous events of Delaware history, like the ride of Caesar Rodney with the whimsical song "Don't Take Him for Granite." (Courtesy of Junior League of Wilmington, Inc.)

JULIE HARRIS. No stranger to the Wilmington stage, actress Julie Harris appeared in six Playhouse productions, including the dramas *I Am a Camera* (1953) and *The Country Wife* (1957) and comedies like *Driving Miss Daisy* (1988). Harris was one of two actresses who celebrated her birthday at the theater when Playhouse staff hosted a party in the theater lobby during the 1992 production of *Lettice and Lovage*. (Courtesy of DT.)

CAROL CHANNING. Carol Channing first appeared at the Playhouse in 1954 when she starred in the production of *Wonderful Town*, by Joseph Fields and Jerome Chodorov. However, she was more famous when she returned in 1977 and earned top billing for her role in *Hello Dolly!* Traveling in the company of her husband and personal manager, she was described by one theater manager as very gracious. (Courtesy of DT.)

LOUIS ARMSTRONG. Photographer Lawrence C. Gropp captured this candid picture of Louis Armstrong on December 1, 1967. Backstage access was very relaxed in the 1960s, so when Gropp and a friend, both photographers, asked whether they could visit Armstrong in the dressing rooms, they were ushered right upstairs. Armstrong graciously allowed them to take photographs of him practicing before his Playhouse concert. (Courtesy of Elaine Gropp; photograph by Lawrence C. Gropp.)

HAIR. Wilmington eyebrows went up when the Playhouse introduced the first burlesque show and production with nudity. The scandalous performances of *Ballet Africanes* and *This Was Burlesque* in the 1960s and 1970s made ticket buyers blush. *Hair*, the first production that contained nudity, showed it only a brief moment, subtly achieved with soft lighting. (Courtesy of HML.)

Three

INTERMISSION
THEATER RENOVATIONS,
DECORATIONS, AND RESERVATIONS

VICTORIAN INTERIOR. Since its opening, the interior has had the elegance of Victorian decor, from the lush velvet fabrics to the gold detailed scrollwork outlining the proscenium. The decorative moldings on top of the columns include a Greek key fret band and border design. A classic egg-and-dart molding, which consists of an oval carved into wood with an arrow-shaped element, defines the design. (Courtesy of DT.)

THE PROSCENIUM. Above the stage and bordering the proscenium is detailed ornamental scroll work. The Greek key fret band design around columns is also carved along the base of the stage. Victorian historic design combines many artistic elements, including Japanese, Celtic, Greek, and Italian Renaissance influences. (Courtesy of DT.)

CHANDELIERS. The original Playhouse chandeliers, shown here, were made in Austria. Not converted to an automatic lowering system to this day, the chandeliers are manually cranked to the floor for cleaning and maintenance. Crystals are individually removed and hand cleaned one by one every year. (Courtesy of DT.)

LUXURIOUS FINISHES. The primary lighting on the main floor comes from large crystal chandeliers, while aluminum bronze chandeliers and wall sconces illuminate large perimeter walls and low ceilings. The Greek key fret band design is shown once again behind the wall sconce. The act curtain was made of rich maroon velour, as were heavy drapes that separated the orchestra from the lobby. (Both, courtesy of DT.)

THE SHUBERT IMPROVEMENTS. Redecoration during the Shubert brothers' lease included new carpeting and paint in 1927. In 1928, they added a double steel protective curtain, one of the only of its kind in any Delaware theater, as well as a projection booth in the gallery. The booth construction included calcium lights and a unique ventilation shaft to carry smoke and gases out of the building. (Courtesy of HML.)

EARLY THEATER CORRIDORS. These images show the interior theater entrance as it appeared before 1952. The original corridor included glass doors with the words "Playhouse" etched above each entrance door. The second image shows open metal doors with a backlit Playhouse marquee. In both images, the box office window is located on the right side of the corridor. After DuPont assumed the role as Playhouse operator, management-commissioned renovations included repainting the theater in 1949 and relocating the box office to the left side of the corridor in 1952. (Both, courtesy of HML.)

THEATER LOBBY, 1970s. The theater lobby in the 1970s displayed a black-and-white checkered floor. Because the entrance into the theater from the corridor has a slight incline, patrons coming in when it rained would track in water, resulting in a potential safety hazard for women wearing high heels who might slip on the wet surface. At this time, many of the decorative moldings were covered by Formica. During the summer of 1987, plush carpeting replaced the checkered tile and moldings were restored. (Courtesy of HML.)

CARPETED LOBBY. The carpeted theater lobby is pictured above and below, showing the entrance into the orchestra seats. The image above shows the original lobby. The first drawn curtain on the left hid the private entrance to the Delaware governor's box seats. A private staircase led up to the second level. The illuminated gentlemen's sign led to basement restrooms and a designated smoking lounge. The entrance to the ladies' restrooms and drawing rooms are not pictured here. Straight ahead is a wide staircase leading to the gallery. The image below depicts the renovated lobby as it appeared for the 75th anniversary ribbon-cutting ceremony on September 22, 1987. (Above, courtesy of HML; below, courtesy of DT.)

RESTORED CEILING MOLDINGS. During the first theater lobby remodeling, a modern drop ceiling covered decorative ceiling moldings. During a later renovation, those moldings were uncovered. In this photograph, workmen are backstage restoring the original ceiling moldings that were reinstalled during the 75th-anniversary lobby renovation. (Courtesy of DT.)

THEATER LOBBY RENOVATIONS. This photograph shows the stages of renovation during the summer of 1987. On the far left, custom wood doors with leaded glass are already in place, as are restored decorative ceiling moldings of the original ceiling. New chandeliers hung in the lobby, and fresh paint and new carpeting refurbished the Playhouse. (Courtesy of DT.)

48

NEW LOBBY DESIGNS. This blueprint shows the plans for redesigning the theater lobby in time for the 75th anniversary in 1987. New features like rich velour curtains and bright red carpet in the corridor enhance the sense of luxury as patrons entered the theater lobby. Live plants provided a feeling of warmth and comfort. Elegant wood-framed glass doors replaced existing metal doors. The second image shows the refurbished lobby. Although the original interior Playhouse marquees hung above the doorways, the marquee shown here is further out in the DuPont Building corridor. (Both, courtesy of HML.)

SEATING RENOVATION. In the early 1990s, the theater redesign included replacing the original seats. Shown here is the Playhouse balcony after the removal of the seats. Workers repaired the floors and aisles in preparation for the new seats. Relocation of the aisles and installation of lighting under the chair armrests added safety measures, as did railings leading down to the front-row seats on the balcony and mezzanine levels. The second image shows the balcony covered in plastic during construction as seen from the stage. (Both, courtesy of DT.)

SAFETY-COMPLIANT UPGRADES. An accessibility study in 1992 identified improvements to ensure the Playhouse complied with safety regulations as well as the special needs of some patrons. Because the theater has no elevator, all handicap-accessible seats are located on the orchestra level. Compliancy required one handicap-accessible seat for every 100 seats. These two seats show one area identified for improvement. Today, all back-row seats in the orchestra are free-standing to facilitate removal and to accommodate a wheelchair or scooter. Other safety improvements included lower railings leading to the mezzanine and balcony levels to meet the recommended 34 to 38 inches for added protection. (Above, courtesy of HML; right, courtesy of DT.)

ORIGINAL AUDITORIUM CEILING.
The original cream ceiling,
accented with gold trim, remained
unchanged from the Playhouse's
opening on October 15, 1913, until
September 1996. (Courtesy of DT.)

NEW SKY MURAL. In the summer of 1996, the Playhouse ceiling underwent a transformation from the traditional cream paint to an elegant sky mural. Scaffolding with stairways throughout the entire auditorium provided a safety feature for the workers, who would not have to climb ladders during the lengthy project. Draping the crystal chandeliers protected them in their places. A team of six to eight workers hand-painted the mural, which they completed in eight weeks. Playgoers first viewed their artistry at the opening of the 1996–1997 season. (Both, courtesy of DT.)

NEW RIGGING AND FLY SPACE. In the early 1990s, manufacturer J.R. Clancey installed new rigging to upgrade the weight capacity in the fly space. The equipment can lift up to 1,000 pounds of scenery or equipment with 60 counterweight battens. Backstage crews operate it from the stage level or the fly floor. (Courtesy of DT.)

FIREPROOF CURTAIN. One life safety improvement made in the early 1990s was the installation of a DuPont Nomex® fiber fireproof curtain. Sensors above the stage trigger the curtain to automatically drop in the event of fire or smoke. Crews can operate this curtain mechanically from stage left or right. (Courtesy of DT.)

TECHNOLOGICAL IMPROVEMENTS. In 1983, the installation of an innovative infrared hearing system with headsets allows the hearing-impaired to enjoy performances. Today, all patrons can clearly hear the show, regardless of their location. Patrons were also pleased with introduction of ordering tickets by phone. (Courtesy of DT.)

GREEN ROOM. Many actors through the years have enjoyed the Hotel du Pont Green Room, which features exquisite French cuisine in an elegant, intimate setting, before or after their performances. Famous singer and actress Rosalind Russell received a standing ovation there following her appearance in the 1956 production of *Auntie Mame*. She said it was the first time that she ever received a standing ovation in a restaurant. (Courtesy of DT.)

CHRISTINA ROOM. The Christina Room in the hotel offered dinner theater packages. The dining room had a secret doorway that opened to the theater lobby, accommodating patrons who enjoyed cocktails and conversation in an adjacent location during intermission. Today, the doorway is sealed, but the keyhole remains visible. (Courtesy of DT.)

SODA SHOP. The Hotel du Pont Soda Shop, originally located in the hotel lobby, offered lunch or a light meal and beverage before Playhouse matinees. Longtime subscribers recall that the Soda Shop provided a prime location for starstruck fans to wait, hoping to catch a glimpse of celebrities after a show. (Courtesy of DT.)

SHIPLEY GRILL. Located only 50 yards from the Playhouse, the Shipley Grill opened in 1950 as the Town House Restaurant. The 90-seat restaurant included a 40-foot marble bar with soda fountain and revolving stools, contrasting with dark tongue-and-groove paneling. New owner Sean Reilly changed the name to Anthony's on Shipley Street in the 1980s. From 1950 to 2001, table 37 was reserved for the stars who dined there, including Kathleen Turner, Vincent Gardenia, Rosie O'Donnell, and others. Restaurant owner Reilly recalls that Turner ordered a Stoli on the rocks after her Saturday matinee performance in *Cat on a Hot Tin Roof.* He said, "She was the most gorgeous woman I ever met in my whole life!" (Both, courtesy of Sean Reilly.)

Four

TAKE A BOW
SPECIAL EVENTS,
ANNIVERSARIES, AND AWARDS

NYLONS POSTCARD. In the late 1930s, a team of scientists at the DuPont Experimental Station announced the development of nylon. Relishing its durability and elasticity, women lined up in stores awaiting an opportunity to purchase their first pairs of nylon stockings. This postcard, used to market Playhouse events, shows performers' legs in nylon stockings, an outstanding representation of a DuPont product used in live theater. (Courtesy of DT.)

ORIGINAL FOUNDERS. Pierre S. du Pont (left) and John J. Raskob, two founders of the Playhouse, are photographed at Longwood Gardens around 1954. Longwood Gardens, a horticultural center founded by du Pont, showcases his other favorite pastime, which was gardening. (Courtesy of HML.)

THE PLAYHOUSE 75TH ANNIVERSARY. On September 22, 1987, the Playhouse announced 75 seasons of Broadway entertainment at a press conference and dedication of the newly renovated lobby. Theater manager Greg Moore and Tim Conway, star of the 75th-season show *The Odd Couple*, offered details about the renovation, announced the 1987–1988 season, and introduced a keepsake book as well as a new Playhouse logo. (Courtesy of HML.)

NEW LOBBY UNVEILING. From left to right, Wilmington mayor Daniel S. Frawley, actor Tim Conway, and general manager Greg Moore participated in the Playhouse ribbon-cutting ceremony moments before revealing the Playhouse lobby renovations. Highlights included a history wall showcasing theater memorabilia from 75 seasons. Historic mementos include construction photographs, original playbills, artifacts from the stage, and a reproduction of the opening-night poster from the first show, *Bought and Paid For.* (Courtesy of DT.)

PLAYHOUSE LONDON SWEEPSTAKES. In 1988, the Playhouse offered each subscriber a chance to win a trip to London to ring in the New Year. The complimentary six-day, seven-night trip for two included round-trip airfare, accommodations at a luxury hotel, and tickets to the hottest shows in London. Actress Jean Stapleton (left) and general manager Greg Moore (right) present the award to Terri Quinn. (Courtesy of DT.)

THEATER WEEK. During the 75th-anniversary season, Mayor Daniel S. Frawley also officially declared May 31, 1988, as "Theater Week" in the City of Wilmington, recognizing the value live theater brings to the city and its residents. At a reception, Mayor Frawley presented the proclamation to Broadway star Chita Rivera and stated that the Playhouse boosts the economy and employs many local residents. *Can-Can*, opening that evening, starred Chita Rivera and the Radio City Music Hall Rockettes. (Courtesy of DT.)

CHILDREN'S SERIES. In 1988, Playhouse staff member Sara Lu Schwartz introduced the Children's Series. It offers schoolchildren from preschool through eighth grade the joys of theater at an affordable price. Engaging more than 40,000 children per year, the program delivers both education and entertainment. Shows vary from biographical musicals about Harriet Tubman to classic kids' books, such as *Are You My Mother?* One school principal said, "My students repeatedly have mentioned how they felt like celebrities when they arrived at the theater!" Schwartz received a DuPont Marketing Excellence Award for her creative efforts. (Right, courtesy of HML; below, courtesy of DT.)

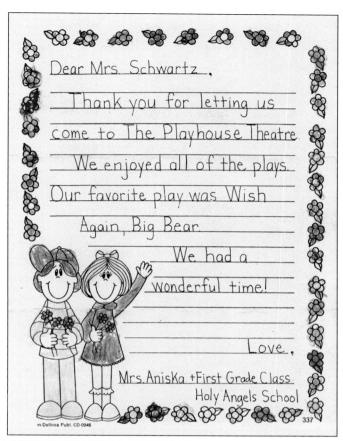

Dear Mrs. Schwartz,
Thank you for letting us come to The Playhouse Theatre. We enjoyed all of the plays. Our favorite play was Wish Again, Big Bear.
We had a wonderful time!
Love,
Mrs. Aniska + First Grade Class
Holy Angels School

Board the Bus!

THE PLAYHOUSE Children's Series

1997-98 Season

78 Consecutive Seasons. Polly Holliday and Charles Durning, stars in the 1990 *Cat on a Hot Tim Roof* production, presented a recognition award from the League of American Theatres and Producers for 78 consecutive seasons to Playhouse general manager Greg Moore (center). The league in New York said, "The Playhouse has always been a favorite stop for Broadway show producers and performers alike. What the Playhouse has accomplished in their market in the past few years has been key in making Broadway a national industry." Moore attributed this success to DuPont support and commitment to the arts, as well as the patrons' continued loyalty, even in difficult years. (Courtesy of HML.)

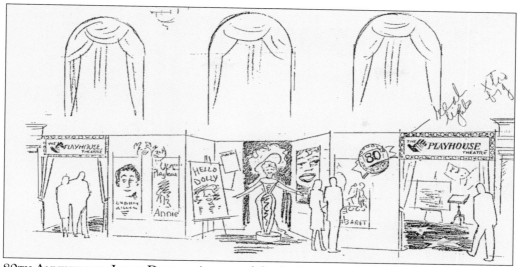

80TH ANNIVERSARY LOBBY DISPLAY. A memorabilia display to commemorate the Playhouse's 80th anniversary was unveiled in the main lobby of the Hotel du Pont in August 1992. The exhibit highlighted 80 years of stars and shows with original playbills, posters, and artifacts, including mannequins dressed in costumes from *Cats* and *Hello Dolly!* The celebration also included a 20-minute historical tour of the dressing rooms, auditorium, scenery, and theater lobby. The Hotel Lobby Lounge offered a Broadway buffet featuring themed dishes and Broadway show tunes. The 80th-anniversary events were open to the public and were frequently visited by Playhouse patrons, DuPont employees, hotel guests, and Wilmington residents. (Both, courtesy of DT.)

100 YEARS OF BROADWAY. Theater manager Patricia Dill (left) stands with box office employees and sales staff in the Playhouse lobby. They are wearing specially designed shirts that commemorate 100 years of New York City Broadway. In the early 1990s, staff members also wore "It's Showtime" shirts during shows. However, for the Broadway milestone in 1993, the uniform celebrated New York theaters. Behind the team is a poster announcing one of the biggest shows of the Playhouse 1993–1994 season, the musical classic *Camelot*, staring Robert Goulet. (Courtesy of HML.)

TOURING CABARET GROUP. From left to right, box office employees Tina Sheing, Diana Milburn, and Cara Johnson Stanard applied their passion for theater and music to organizing a traveling theater trio group. During the theater off-season, they performed cabarets at various schools, retirement communities, and local businesses within a three-hour radius to market upcoming Playhouse seasons. Milburn remembers performing one of their cabarets at a sister hospitality property, the DuPont Country Club, for a group of DuPont executives. (Courtesy of DT.)

THE PLAYHOUSE THEATRE

cordially invites you to join us on

Thursday, April 17, 1997 at 10:30 a.m.

for a press reception and live performance

celebrating the start of

our 85th Anniversary Season

at The Playhouse Theatre

Du Pont Building

10th and Market Streets

Wilmington, Delaware

R.S.V.P. Diana Hunt 302.594.3192 by April 14th

85TH ANNIVERSARY. Press, staff, and VIPs received this invitation welcoming them to a reception to commemorate the 85th-anniversary season. The "ghost" of leading Playhouse actress Alice Brady, daughter of the first Playhouse Theatre lessee, greeted them. She graced the stage in a special theater tribute written and performed by professional opera soprano and Playhouse staff member Diana Milburn. After the performance, guests attended backstage group tours and a reception. Continuing the celebration throughout the season, patrons enjoyed similar complimentary lunchtime cabarets and backstage tours. The 85th season included the shows *Stomp, Annie, Big,* and *Cirque Ingenieux.* (Courtesy of DT.)

KIDS DAY ON BROADWAY. Playhouse employee Sara Lu Schwartz poses in a Lucy cardboard cutout, a prop used for the Playhouse production *Kids Day on Broadway* in 1999. Children participated in face painting, arts and crafts, karaoke, and a special lunch in the Hotel du Pont Grill before attending the 30th-anniversary production of *You're A Good Man, Charlie Brown*, starring Roger Bart, Kristin Chenoweth, Anthony Rapp, and B.D. Wong. Schwartz created the Children's Series and other marketing initiatives, including lobby lounge lunches followed by backstage tours, which raised awareness of the Playhouse within the community. (Courtesy of DT.)

SPECIALTY RENTAL EVENTS. In addition to live theater, the Playhouse stage has hosted nontheatrical events, including lectures, art exhibits, and even a wedding. In the late 1990s, one local bank requested use of the stage for its annual dinner for more than 300 guests. Accommodating the request required enlarging the stage, which involved removing the seats. Scaffolding, aluminum beams, and decking formed a bridge over remaining orchestra seats. Finally, workmen lay the stage extension on the decking and tested it before setting up the event. (Both, courtesy of DT.)

CHAMPIONS ON ICE. The stage crew transformed the Playhouse stage into an ice-skating rink for *Champions on Ice*. They poured 10,000 pounds of crushed ice into a rubber deck approximately 36 feet deep by 40 feet wide with raised sides. They continuously watered down the surface until it froze. A tractor trailer flatbed with a refrigeration unit temporarily installed cooling lines in the theater, freezing the water until the ice was approximately three and a half inches thick. After the show, the crews turned off the cooling unit and used sledgehammers to break up the ice. They transported wheelbarrows of ice to the courtyards to dissipate. Former Playhouse technical director Terry Gray describes this as one of his most unusual but rewarding projects. He even brought his children to the show. (Courtesy of DT.)

PLAYHOUSE EXTERIOR. Banners commemorating the 85th season graced the Playhouse exterior on Market Street. They included the Playhouse's earned moniker "Wilmington's Little Broadway" as well as architectural column designs prominent in the Playhouse interior. Hanging from the marquee is the banner for *Big*, the 1997–1998 season opener. (Courtesy of DT.)

SMART TALK SERIES. In the year 2000, a Canadian-based organization called Unique Lives visited the Playhouse looking for a venue for its celebrity-based series. The program offered theater patrons a series of intimate lectures from inspirational women, including actresses, authors, doctors, first ladies, and others. Not only were the visitors impressed with the size, they loved the luxurious adjoining hotel for their female guest speakers, and the organization has reserved the Playhouse ever since. In 2002, the series adopted a new name, Smart Talk, to expand the demographic of guest speakers. Mary Tyler Moore, Barbara Bush, Goldie Hawn, Debbie Reynolds, Delaware native Valerie Bertinelli, and Diane Keaton are among the remarkable women who came to share their lives with theater audiences. (Both, courtesy of DT.)

DuPont^{SM} THEATRE

THE DUPONT THEATRE. On February 28, 2003, the Playhouse adopted a new name, DuPont^{SM} Theatre. Including "At the Hotel du Pont" as part of its logo, the theater highlights its unique location within a world-class hotel. Changing the name to DuPont Theatre also links the theater to fellow hospitality properties, the Hotel du Pont and the DuPont Country Club. Adding the service mark strengthens its ties to the company brand. (Courtesy of DT.)

90TH ANNIVERSARY. To commemorate the DuPont Theatre's 90th anniversary, Hotel du Pont executive pastry chef Michele Mitchell baked a specialty cake. Her objective was to create a cake inspired by the historic wall display that graces the theater lobby. Mitchell replicated several exhibits on the sides of this pyramid cake. (Courtesy of Michele Mitchell.)

Wilmington Ballet
Academy of the Dance est. 1956

The Nutcracker

Guest Principal Dancers Michele Wiles and
Cory Stearns of American Ballet Theatre

Dancers of the Sandonato School of Ballet

Wilmington Ballet Orchestra,
Allan R. Scott, conducting

Music: Pytor Tchaikovsky

Choreography: Jorge Laico & Barbara Sandonato

December 19 - 20, 2009

DUPONT THEATRE • WILMINGTON, DELAWARE 19801

THE NUTCRACKER. On December 15, 2006, the Academy of the Dance in Wilmington presented a plaque of recognition for 40 years of dedicated commitment to the academy productions of *The Nutcracker*. This classic holiday ballet is traditionally paired with a Nutcracker Afternoon Tea in the Hotel du Pont Lobby Lounge. (Courtesy of DT.)

IT'S NOT MEAN TO BE GREEN. Retired Children's Series coordinator Barbara Slavin partnered with local Wilmington author Jamie Kleman to create a children's musical based on Kleman's book *It's Not Mean to be Green.* In April 2010, the DuPont Theatre featured the world premiere of this musical production about caring for Mother Earth. It traces the journey of Michael McDurth—a young boy confused by the common phrase "go green." Kleman, executive director of A Bigger Boat Foundation, is working with Slavin, Jim Tristani, TribeSound Records, and Film Brothers to take their music and message to the screen in an animated version of *It's Not Mean to be Green.* This earth-friendly special will be suitable for use in homes and schools across the country to spark Green Team initiatives. (Courtesy of Jamie Kleman; photographs by Kerry Angell.)

Five

BACKSTAGE PASS
OPERATING A SHOW
BEHIND THE CURTAIN

GHOST LIGHT. The theater ghost light glows from center stage as a safety warning that no one is permitted on the stage. In theater tradition, a ghost light is illuminated when the theater is not in use. One traditional explanation is that the light prevents someone from falling into the orchestra pit, but a superstitious explanation is that the light is left on for the theater's ghost. (Courtesy of HML.)

THEATER LOAD-IN. A theater load-in requires precision and teamwork to ensure that scenery, costumes, props, and equipment are safely and efficiently set up in time for a performance. It begins with a spotting call the evening before the show opens, when a production member measures and lays out the rigging equipment. On the morning of the opening performance, up to six tractor trailers arrive for stagehands to unload. It takes approximately eight hours to load in a show. (Courtesy of DT.)

STAGEHANDS. From 20 to 75 stagehands are involved in loading in a show for the DuPont Theatre Broadway Series, depending on its size. From six to 25 stagehands operate equipment during the show. Six department heads manage the load-in, including a carpenter, flyman, wardrobe mistress, soundman, props master, and lighting technician. (Courtesy of DT.)

Toolbox Talk. A safety meeting, known as "toolbox talk," takes place before every load-in to review procedures, personal protective equipment, and more. For example, DuPont requires anyone on stage during a load-in to wear a hard hat. Safety pocket cards like this one serve as reminder to employees and out-of-town production staff that safety is the number-one priority in this theater. (Courtesy of DT.)

THE PLAYHOUSE THEATRE
At DuPont, safety is our #1 priority.

1. Housekeeping — Pick up unnecessary materials, trash, etc.
2. Use the proper tool for the job.
3. Know what to do, who to call, and what your rally points are in an emergency.
4. Don't stand under a moving load.
5. Never touch an unstable load on a forklift.
6. No lighted smoking materials allowed while working.
7. Wear gloves/safety glasses when appropriate.
8. Take two; plan the job.
9. Safety is everyone's responsibility. Be aware of your surroundings.
10. Report all incidents and injuries to your supervisor.

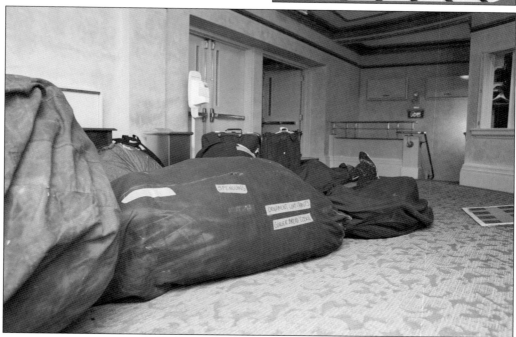

Pre-Production Lobby. The theater lobby serves as a multifunctional space during a production load-in. Labeled costume bags and props arrive in the lobby before distribution to labeled dressing rooms. Orchestra members use the lobby for rehearsal before the show. (Courtesy of DT.)

FIRE DOORS. Two fire doors separate the stage from the principal and ensemble dressing rooms. During a theater load-in, the fire doors are often opened, as oversized costume trunks need access through these doors to the first- and second-floor dressing rooms. Stairwells are too narrow to accommodate oversized items safely. (Courtesy of DT.)

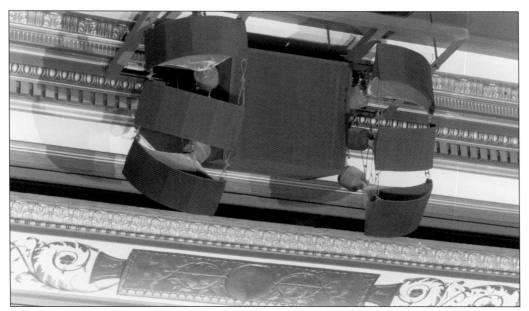

SPEAKER SYSTEM. The Playhouse sound system is comprised of three main speakers. This center speaker cluster hangs directly over center stage and fills the balcony, mezzanine, and orchestra with sound. To the left and right of the proscenium, speakers are built into the wall. A sound booth in the back of the orchestra seating controls volume and is capable of producing up to 105 decibels. (Courtesy of DT.)

LIGHTING. When the Playhouse opened in 1913, the lighting switchboard was state of the art, one of the safest and most modern systems in the United States. Stage illumination included 816 incandescent lights, and the switchboard had 3,000 connections for wires. The dead-face system prevented shock if the operator were to come in contact with the panel. Today, 192 dimmers and 173 lighting units offer equal state-of-the-art capability. (Courtesy of DT.)

COSTUME LOAD-IN. Prop master Raymond Harrington supervises lowering oversized costume trunks into the basement dressing rooms during a production load-in. This procedure includes removing planks from the theater stage floor and chaining off the opening before work begins. The bins are securely attached to a rig and automatically lowered to a second stagehand waiting in the basement. After releasing the trunks from their harness, costume bins are distributed to the wardrobe team. (Courtesy of DT.)

WARDROBE TEAM. A position on the wardrobe team requires grace under pressure. The department head is responsible for matching local and traveling production dressers with cast members to ensure all costume needs occur at the right moment during performances. General tasks include last-minute costume stitching, arranging for dry cleaning and shoe repair, costume changes, steaming, and more. Many interested theater lovers inquire about working on the wardrobe team in hopes of seeing Broadway shows; however, this fast-paced work prevents any free time to watch a live production from backstage. (Courtesy of DT.)

WARDROBE MAINTENANCE. Wardrobe crises—wear and tear, broken zippers, runs in stockings, rips in clothing, and missing costume pieces—occur often. The wardrobe staff must act quickly and think creatively. Wardrobe supervisor Eva Lynne Penn remembers when an actress got a run in her black stockings before going on stage. Not having time to find replacements, Penn jokingly offered to paint over the run with a black marker. She added, "I'm literally backstage with my notes around my neck. It's definitely not as glamorous as it may appear." Her team makes special preparations for dance productions. "Dancing eight performances is hard on a costume. Those shows usually require extra costume maintenance." (Both, courtesy of DT.)

ACTORS IN COSTUME. The captain in the 1991 musical *Titanic* and dancers from the 1998 *Cirque Ingenieux* pose in costume before appearing on the stage. Wardrobe employees say that once the actors are in their costumes, the show truly begins backstage. In costume, actors become their characters, walking up and down the hallways running lines and singing songs, complete with accents and character names. Wardrobe supervisor Eva Lynne Penn recalls "gangsters" Joseph Mascolo and Vince Viverito completely in character, entertaining the dressers backstage during the production of *Breaking Legs*. (Both, courtesy of Eva Lynne Penn.)

CATS MAKEUP. Film crews captured an actor transforming himself into his feline makeup for the Playhouse production of *Cats* in January 1988. This production was unusual because all cast members were responsible for doing their own hair and makeup. One local school arranged a field trip to the theater to watch the actress playing Grizabella transform herself from a human into a cat. (Both, courtesy of HML.)

PRESIDENTIAL SEAL. Stage crews prepare the theater for a speech by Pres. George W. Bush in 2007. President Bush was in Wilmington during a visit to a Wilmington DuPont site, the Experimental Station. It was a privilege for the stage crew to capture this photograph of the Presidential Seal positioned on the podium during preparations. Although it is normally the last item to be placed on the podium before the president takes the stage, the closely monitored seal was tested in advance to ensure its visibility under the special stage lighting. (Both, courtesy of Raymond Harrington.)

SAND AND WATER. To conform to DuPont's safety regulations, a bucket of sand, a bucket of water, and a fire extinguisher must be placed in the left and right box seats at every DuPont shareholders meeting. In addition, a Wilmington city firefighter must be present to monitor the items during the meeting. (Both, courtesy of DT.)

DRESSING ROOMS. When it opened in 1913, the Playhouse had 20 dressing rooms on two levels. Today, all dressing rooms comply with equity codes, which include a makeup table, mirror, and sink. Equity also requires a cot for the actors to use if needed. For musicals and dance productions, ensemble cast members share large chorus rooms. All principal actors have a rider, a list of specially requested items for their dressing rooms. These requests have included adding a private bath and shower or a piano in their room or specifying a particular brand of bottled water or soap. (Right, courtesy of HML; below, courtesy of DT.)

DRESSING ROOM DESIGN CONTEST. Several dressing rooms were renovated in 1987 for the 75th anniversary, but dressing room No. 9 received special star treatment in 2005. The production lead earns the room equipped with a full bathroom, including a shower stall. Theater staff collaborated with college students at the Delaware School of Art and Design in a dressing room design contest. With a budget of $1,000, one lucky student won the opportunity to make over a dressing room, which he did with fresh paint, new accessories, new lighting, and reupholstered furniture. Julie Andrews was the first actress to use this remodeled room during her production of *The Boy Friend*. (Both, courtesy of DT.)

SESAME STREET. DuPont Theatre wardrobe mistress Eva Lynne Penn shares the challenges involved in dressing the cast of *Sesame Street*. Each costume has a very specific maintenance schedule inside it, and the costumes are heavy and hot. Tables are set up backstage and lined with fans to cool the characters down between appearances. While in the costumes, actors have very limited vision, with only a dark, peripheral view. Unlike other shows that require dressers to wear black, *Sesame Street* productions allow the dressers to wear bright colors to increase visibility. All backstage entrances are draped in black to protect the illusion that these are the real stars of Sesame Street, not actors in costume. (Both, courtesy of Eva Lynne Penn.)

MERCHANDISE CART. The DuPont hospitality maintenance team built this merchandise cart staffed by a theater concession employee. It is standard for Broadway productions to provide their own merchandise to sell before the show, during intermission, and after the show. (Courtesy of Nancy McKewen.)

USHERS UNIFORMS. The original usherettes wore uniforms consisting of black skirts with white blouses that they provided. Over time, their uniform colors changed to navy blue skirts with yellow blouses, but they still purchased them. By the 1980s, uniforms of black tuxedo skirts, white tuxedo shirts, and black bow ties were provided by theater management. Today, the uniform is black slacks and a black dress shirt. (Courtesy of Nancy McEwen.)

THE
PLAYHOUSE
THEATRE

Presents

| SAL MINEO | KEVIN McCARTHY | RALPH MEEKER |

in

SOMETHING ABOUT A SOLDIER

USHERETTE EXPERIENCE. Former Playhouse usherette Marjorie McNinch recounts her experiences from 1961. She cannot forget how starstruck she was when she met Sal Mineo in *Something about a Soldier*. "I didn't faint, but I was close to it," she admits. McNinch also recalls that Rex Harrison had a "presence that was unmistakable." She still owns the vinyl record of the Playhouse's 1964 premiere of *The Roar of the Greasepaint, the Smell of the Crowd*, starring Anthony Newly. In her late teens, McNinch, the youngest usherette, felt privileged to see shows she might never have seen otherwise. Her responsibilities included showing patrons to their seats, pointing out the nearest safety exits, and handing out programs. "Working with the public taught me to be diplomatic," she says. (Both, courtesy of HML.)

THE
PLAYHOUSE
THEATRE

PRESENTS

THE ROAR OF THE GREASEPAINT -THE SMELL OF THE CROWD

WALLS OF FAME. Initiated by the DuPont Theatre stagehands, several prominent backstage walls of fame boast signatures of famous show people. Some actually inscribed their names on the brick walls of the stage. Over time, as paint started to chip and fade, the signatures began to deteriorate. The crew then decided to use large white boards that could be preserved. They located one white board for autographs on the first floor of the theater, across the hall from the principals' dressing rooms. Signers include Connie Chung, Rita McKenzie, Isabella Rossellini, Sidney Poitier, and others. Even Pres. George W. Bush signed an unoccupied wall on the stage, a space one of his aides scouted out especially for him. (Both, courtesy of DT.)

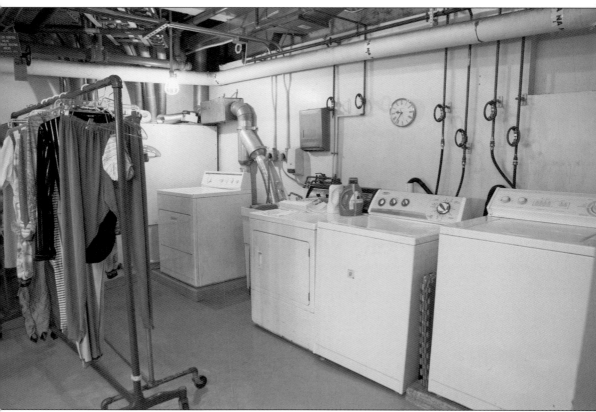

LAUNDRY FACILITIES. Washers and dryers in the basement of the DuPont Theatre offered convenience to the wardrobe staff that travel with a show. Often, a production troupe heads to the theater following an evening performance in a neighboring state. After packing up the costumes, props, and sets, crews drive overnight to Wilmington. Members of the wardrobe staff have the responsibility for laundering all costumes in time for the next evening performance. The soft water system in the theater limits the amount of detergent needed. For specialty items that cannot be washed and dried in the theater, wardrobe staff arranges for local dry cleaning. (Courtesy of DT.)

THE ORCHESTRA PIT.

Through this small square doorway, just large enough to accommodate a tuba, the crew loads instruments into the orchestra pit. Located below the stage overhang, pit capacity allows for 20 to 25 musicians. Only the conductor can see the stage; the instrumentalists cannot observe the performance above. The orchestra pit was extended by approximately three feet in 1990 to accommodate larger shows. Most productions specify a conductor, pianist, and a drummer in the contract; locally recruited musicians with very little time to practice make up the rest of the orchestra. They must be able to effortlessly switch among a variety of different musical genres at a fast pace. (Above, courtesy of DT; right, courtesy of HML.)

THE "IT" DOOR. The theater basement contains a crawlspace called the plenum which leads to an underground tunnel from the stage to the sound booth. Its narrow dimensions force workmen running cables to lie on a wheeled cart and pull their way through the tunnel. The metal doorway that leads to the plenum was nicknamed the "It" door by stage hands in reference to a similar doorway from Stephen King's book-turned-television mini-series *It.* Coincidentally, Richard Thomas, who starred in the mini-series, was performing in *12 Angry Men* when he stumbled upon the "It" door. Recognizing the printed symbol on the door from his earlier role, he took photographs in front of it and autographed them for several employees. (Above, courtesy of DT; left, courtesy of Raymond Harrington.)

THE PLAYHOUSE THEATRE
at the Hotel du Pont

big

September 26 - October 5, 1997

STAGE CREW AS EXTRAS. It is not uncommon for a show to incorporate the stage crew in live performances. One dresser hid onstage in a set elevator during the 1997 production of *Big* so that she could dress an actor. Another went down with a sinking ship in *Dr. Doolittle*. For *Blue Man Group*, stagehands were fitted with special jumpsuits for each performance, because they appeared on stage in several skits. (Courtesy of DT.)

THE BOX OFFICE. Box office employees are responsible for selling 10,000 tickets per show. Until 1986, tickets were still racked. A ticket vendor printed and delivered tickets to the box office employees approximately three weeks before a show. Staff sorted them by hand in proper rows, seats, and locations. Patrons could order tickets by phone, mail, or in person, but they had to pick up their tickets at the box office window. (Courtesy of HML.)

Six

ENCORE

STORIES, STARS, AND SHOWS FROM 1987 TO TODAY

CHITA RIVERA. Tony Award–winner Chita Rivera is no stranger to celebrating theater anniversaries in Wilmington. She first appeared at the Playhouse in the 1988 season finale production of *Can-Can*, a musical starring the Radio City Music Hall Rockettes. She returned to the Playhouse stage for the 85th-anniversary celebration in *Chita and All that Jazz*. (Courtesy of DT.)

MITZI GAYNOR. Wilmington restaurant owner Sean Reilly recounts several appearances by Mitzi Gaynor, leading star in 1989's *Anything Goes*. When she walked in his restaurant, the Shipley Grill, fellow diners stood and applauded. He remembers her as so gracious, smiling and bowing to her fans and then greeting dining patrons before her meal. Reilly shares that before her shows, she always ordered a salad for lunch. After her shows, she always ordered fois gras and a bottle of Mondavi Fumé Blanc for her dinner. Sharing a copy of his autographed menu, Reilly raves, "She was a star, the way a star should be!" (Both, courtesy of Sean Reilly.)

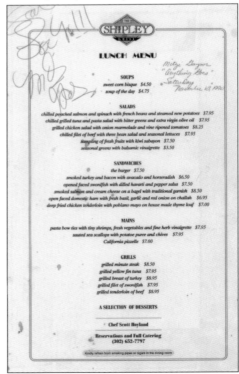

HALLOWEEN CHILDREN'S SERIES. Children visited the Playhouse dressed in Halloween costumes for *American Sampler*, a children's production staged on October 31, 1989. For many students, the trip to the Playhouse was their first theater experience. Retired Children's Series coordinator Barbara Slavin shared two commonly asked questions from visiting students, "Do you live here?" and "Are those chandeliers made of diamonds?" (Courtesy of HML.)

KATHLEEN TURNER. Kathleen Turner appeared at the Playhouse in the 1990s *Cat on a Hot Tin Roof*. In the audience was Turner's friend and popular musician Billy Joel. According to theater staff, one patron asked Turner to sign her husband's graduation cap from Northwestern University. Her husband and Turner were in the same acting class. (Courtesy of DT.)

VINCENT GARDENIA. Vincent Gardenia was no stranger to Wilmington during his appearance in 1992's *Breaking Legs*. Playhouse staff shared stories of his frequent walks down Market Street between shows. On one occasion, a fan approached him outside the Woolworth store at Ninth and Market Streets. When asked if he were "that guy from the movies," he responded that no he wasn't but "I get that a lot." During his visit, he visited several local restaurants, Shipley Grill and Cavanaugh's on Market Street among others. Because he loved cooking so much, he even collaborated with the management at Cavanaugh's to prepare a special dinner in their kitchen, to the enjoyment of several Playhouse employees. (Left, courtesy of HML; below, courtesy of Sean Reilly.)

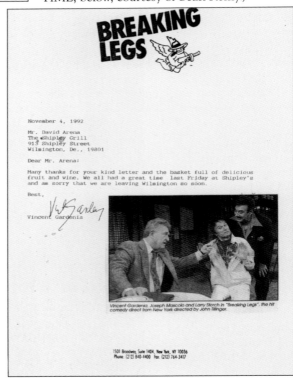

November 4, 1992

Mr. David Arena
The Shipley Grill
913 Shipley Street
Wilmington, De., 19801

Dear Mr. Arena:

Many thanks for your kind letter and the basket full of delicious fruit and wine. We all had a great time last Friday at Shipley's and am sorry that we are leaving Wilmington so soon.

Best,

Vincent Gardenia

Vincent Gardenia, Joseph Mascolo and Larry Storch in "Breaking Legs", the hit comedy direct from New York directed by John Tillinger.

1501 Broadway, Suite 1404, New York, NY 10036
Phone: (212) 840-4400 Fax: (212) 764-3417

Rosie O'Donnell. Rosie O'Donnell made her theater debut as Rizzo in *Grease* at the Playhouse in 1993. Playhouse employees and their families attended a private dress rehearsal and received strict instruction not to applaud during the rehearsal. After the performance, Rosie teased the audience asking, "Didn't you like the show? Why didn't anyone clap?" She graciously signed every child's playbill after the private performance. Theater staff described her as very motherly, showing extreme support and a concern for other actors and ensemble members in the production. (Courtesy of DT.)

LORETTA SWIT. Actress Loretta Swit participated in a Playhouse press conference before her one-woman show, *Shirley Valentine*, in October 1993. Box office and theater employees shared memories of her visits to their offices to say hello and observe them performing simple daily tasks such as answering the phones. One Playhouse assistant manager remembers taking her out shopping on Market Street between performances. (Courtesy of DT.)

ROBERT GOULET BILLBOARD. To promote the 1993–1994 Playhouse Broadway Series, a billboard featuring Robert Goulet in *Camelot* advertised the show on major city street Delaware Avenue in downtown Wilmington. Playhouse employees recall that Goulet was the only Playhouse actor who mailed a holiday card to the staff every year after his appearance. (Courtesy of DT.)

THE SECRET GARDEN PARTY. *The Secret Garden* was the one show included in both the Children's Series and the Broadway Series. To complement the 1993 Broadway production of *The Secret Garden*, the Playhouse collaborated with its sister property, the DuPont Country Club, to host a themed *Secret Garden* dinner party for members at Brantwyn Estate, a former du Pont family private residence located on the country club grounds. Participants enjoyed having a private dinner in a country setting before attending the show. Today, the Brantwyn Estate hosts other private dinners, weddings, social events, and business meetings. (Courtesy of DT; photograph by Clair Pruett Photography.)

JUST FOR LAUGHS. Tim Conway (left) and Tom Poston laugh on the set of 1994's opening show, *Just for Laughs.* Guests and employees had even more laughs when Conway comically appeared at the show's press conference with a long trail of toilet paper coming out of his pants. He entertained in the Hotel du Pont's Green Room restaurant by posing as a waiter with a beverage towel draped over his arm. Theater employees recount that Poston enjoyed his stay at the Hotel du Pont during the run of the show, perhaps because he received many food baskets sent from local restaurateurs who wanted to welcome him to town. He graciously took these baskets to the theater for stagehands to share. (Both, courtesy of HML.)

SUSAN STROMAN. Five-time Tony Award winner and choreographer Susan Stroman is a Wilmington native. She choreographed the national touring show *And the World Goes Round*, which appeared at the Playhouse in 1993. At a Playhouse-hosted reception following the show, her father, Charles H. Stroman, a local pianist in Wilmington, entertained guests. (Courtesy of DT.)

STIEGLITZ LOVES O'KEEFFE. Stacy Keach and Margot Kidder answered questions at a press conference held in the Hotel du Pont on May 11, 1995, about their show, *Flowers and Photos: Stieglitz Loves O'Keeffe*, which depicted the love story of painter Georgia O'Keeffe and photographer Alfred Stieglitz. Their correspondence from 1915 until 1946 included more than 25,000 letters. (Courtesy of HML.)

GREASE, 1995. When Tommy Tune returned with a production of *Grease* in 1995, actor Adrian Zmed, who was cast as Danny Zuko, hurt his ankle during a rehearsal. Ricky Paull Goldin, who played Danny in the 1993 production, agreed to fill in at the last minute. Wardrobe employees remembered that his hair was not long enough for the "greaser" hairstyles; therefore, the production team had his wigs sent on a separate flight. Sally Struthers was in the cast for this tour as well as Debbie Gibson (above), who appeared as Rizzo, the role that Rosie O'Donnell played two years earlier. (Both, courtesy of Eva Lynne Penn.)

Barry & Fran Weissler
Jujamcyn Theaters

present

The **Tommy Tune** Production of

Grease!

Book, Music and Lyrics by

Jim Jacobs *and* **Warren Casey**

starring

Debbie Gibson   Adrian Zmed

as Betty Rizzo   *as Danny Zuko*

Kevin-Anthony   Michelle Bombacie   Erick Buckley
Steve Geyer   Trisha M. Gorman
Lesley Jennings   Beth Lipari
Tom Richter   Ric Ryder   Nick Santa Maria   Amanda Watkins
Marissa Jaret Winokur   Christopher Youngsman

Laura J. Barger   Sutton Foster   Cynthia Gray   Alan Jenkins   Mark Lanyon
Robb McKindles   Stefani Rae   Bill Rolon   Mary Ruvolo
Thomas Scott   Timothy Edward Smith   Steven X. Ward   Joanna Young

Sally Struthers

as Miss Lynch

Scenic Design   *Costume Design*   *Lighting Design*
John Arnone   Willa Kim   Howell Binkley

Hair Design   *Sound Design*   *Associate Choreographer*   *Dance Supervisor*
Patrik D. Moreton   Tom Morse   Jerry Mitchell   Patti D'Beck

Musical Supervision,
Vocal and Dance Arrangements   *Musical Direction*   *Orchestrations*   *Musical Coordinator*
John McDaniel   Michael Biagi   Steve Margoshes   John Monaco

Press Representative   *Casting*
Anita Dloniak   Stuart Howard & Amy Schecter

Production Coordinator   *Production Stage Manager*   *Technical Supervisor*
Craig Jacobs   Bill Roberts   Arthur Siccardi

Presented in Association with
Pace Theatrical Group   TV Asahi

Associate Producer   *General Manager*
Alecia Parker   Charlotte W. Wilcox

Directed and Choreographed by

Jeff Calhoun

Look for the new cast recording on RCA VICTOR

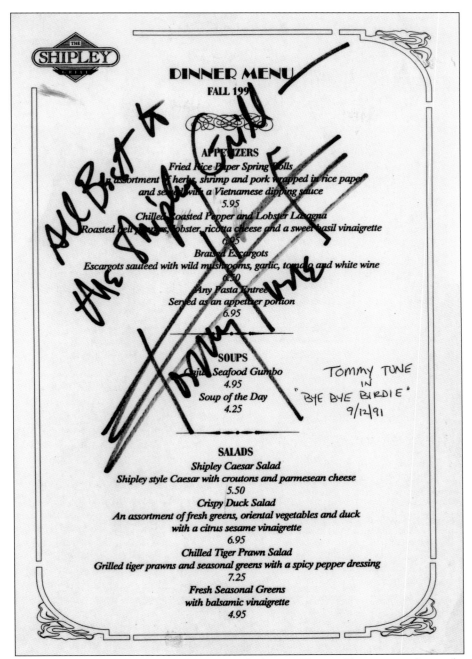

THE SHIPLEY

DINNER MENU
FALL 199[?]

APPETIZERS

Fried Rice Paper Spring Rolls
An assortment of herbs, shrimp and pork wrapped in rice paper
and served with a Vietnamese dipping sauce
5.95

Chilled Roasted Pepper and Lobster Lasagna
Roasted bell peppers, lobster, ricotta cheese and a sweet basil vinaigrette
6.95

Braised Escargots
Escargots sauteed with wild mushrooms, garlic, tomato and white wine
6.50

Any Pasta Entree
Served as an appetizer portion
6.95

SOUPS

Cajun Seafood Gumbo
4.95

Soup of the Day
4.25

TOMMY TUNE
IN
"BYE BYE BIRDIE"
9/12/91

All Best to
The Shipley Grill
Tommy Tune

SALADS

Shipley Caesar Salad
Shipley style Caesar with croutons and parmesean cheese
5.50

Crispy Duck Salad
An assortment of fresh greens, oriental vegetables and duck
with a citrus sesame vinaigrette
6.95

Chilled Tiger Prawn Salad
Grilled tiger prawns and seasonal greens with a spicy pepper dressing
7.25

Fresh Seasonal Greens
with balsamic vinaigrette
4.95

TOMMY TUNE. No stranger to the Wilmington Playhouse, Tommy Tune wrote, directed, acted, produced, and choreographed a variety of shows from 1965 to 2005. In 1991, he was involved in two major productions. In September, he starred in the musical *Bye Bye Birdie*. He also wrote and directed the five-time Tony Award–winning musical *Grand Hotel*, which appeared that November. His noteworthy performances included producing *Grease* and *Dr. Doolittle*, which he both directed and performed a leading role in. A gracious performer, he signed memorabilia, such as this menu for local residents and even one Playhouse dresser's tap shoes. (Courtesy of Sean Reilly.)

THE PLAYHOUSE THEATRE

JAMES WHITMORE IN

BULLY

AN ADVENTURE WITH TEDDY ROOSEVELT

BULLY. *Bully,* a one-man biodrama relating the life of Theodore Roosevelt, appeared twice at the Playhouse. The play included stories, speeches, and letters from Teddy and his friends, family, admirers, and enemies. The first production featured James Whitmore as Roosevelt. The second production in 1998 starred John Davidson. The president's grandson, Theodore Roosevelt III, attended the press conference and opening-night performance. (Courtesy of HML.)

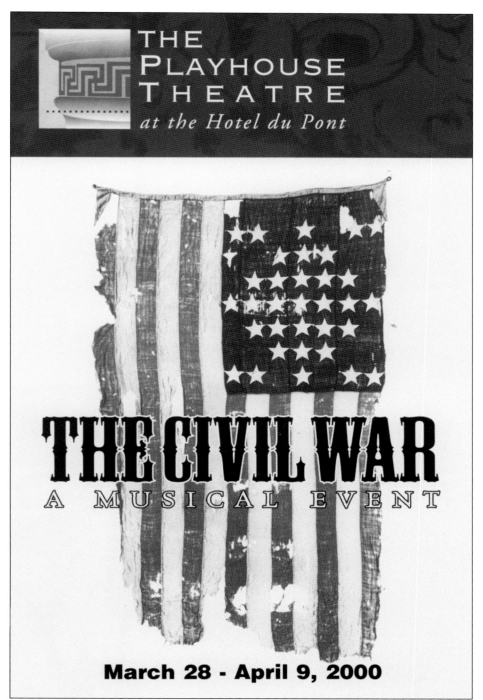

THE
PLAYHOUSE
THEATRE
at the Hotel du Pont

THE CIVIL WAR
A MUSICAL EVENT

March 28 - April 9, 2000

CIVIL WAR. Larry Gatlin appeared at the Playhouse in *Civil War* in March 2000. Theater staff recalled how graciously and humorously he entertained crowds in the theater lobby before the show when a technical problem during the Wednesday matinee kept patrons from entering the theater. He appeared in a bathrobe and sang a song while the problem was resolved. (Courtesy of DT.)

BARBARA EDEN. Actress Barbara Eden graced the Playhouse stage in March 2002 in *The Odd Couple*. One employee recounted that her tasks included calling a local shuttle service to request transportation for Eden. The man on the line calmly said, "Can you hold please?" Forgetting to put the phone on hold, he raved to his coworkers, "I get to pick up the *I Dream of Genie* girl!" (Courtesy of DT.)

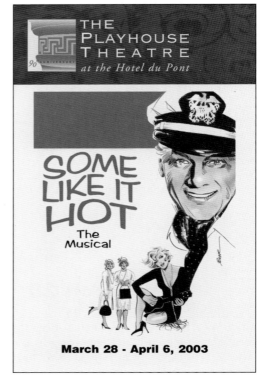

TONY CURTIS. A natural performer, Tony Curtis starred at the Playhouse in 2003 in *Some Like It Hot* but also entertained hotel and theater guests off the stage when he was seen comically wandering around the Hotel du Pont between shows, wearing shorts with snow boots or sitting cross-legged on the hotel's Lobby Lounge floor. (Courtesy of DT.)

IF YOU EVER LEAVE ME. Actor Joe Bologna and his wife Renee Taylor, stars of *If You Ever Leave Me . . . I'm Going with You*, literally could not leave the DuPont Theatre because a snow blizzard in February 2003 forced officials to declare a state of emergency. When the show continued, audiences were especially delighted by the on stage surprise renewal of their wedding vows officiated by New Castle County clerk of the peace Ken Boulden. (Courtesy of DT.)

JULIE ANDREWS'S BIRTHDAY. Actress and director Julie Andrews greets guests at her 70th-birthday celebration in the DuBarry Room at the Hotel du Pont on October 1, 2005, during her visit to Wilmington. Her directing debut for *The Boy Friend* had opened its national tour at the DuPont Theatre on September 30, 2005. At her birthday celebration, Andrews revealed that *The Boy Friend* was such a special project for her because it was her first play in the United States on New York City's Broadway in 1954. (Left, courtesy of Eliane Gropp, photograph by Lawrence C. Gropp; below, courtesy of DT.)

CHILDREN'S CHOIR TRYOUTS. Some productions at the Playhouse, such as *Tommy* and *Handel's Messiah Rocks*, involve the local community in hosting tryouts for children's choirs to join their shows. Two choirs, shown here, audition for the opportunity to be cast in *Joseph and the Amazing Technicolor Dreamcoat*. (Courtesy of DT.)

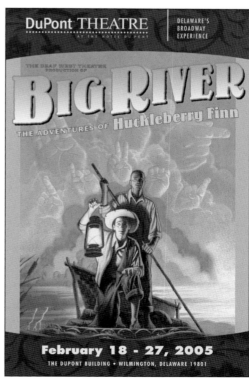

BIG RIVER. *Big River* first appeared at the Playhouse in 1987. The second production in 2005, the Deaf West Theatre production of *Big River*, was particularly poignant because half of the cast was deaf. Some paired with speaking actors who provided their voice, while others relied on reading lips, using television prompters for their cues, and communicating through American Sign Language. (Courtesy of DT.)

FROST/NIXON CAST. DuPont Theatre props master Raymond Harrington snapped this photograph of the *Frost/Nixon* cast. Actor Stacy Keach requested this photograph for a friend who could not attend the performance. It is the responsibility of the prop master to inventory and provide all props needed for a production, including, in this case, a camera for an actor. (Courtesy of Raymond Harrington.)

BILLIE JEAN KING. Tennis members from the DuPont Country Club who work part-time as usherettes at the DuPont Theatre stand with tennis legend Billie Jean King, cofounder of World Team Tennis, after her Smart Talk Series appearance. (Courtesy of Nancy McEwen.)

BERMUDA AVENUE TRIANGLE. DuPont Theatre prop master Raymond Harrington recalls his experience with *Bermuda Avenue Triangle*, a production that he said encompassed true "theater magic." After a leak in storage tractor trailers damaged sets during the drive to the theater, Harrington was asked to build and provide all sets and props just days before the scheduled opening. Working from a list of required props, he even brought items from his own home to decorate the sets, including bamboo curtains and a martini set. During one performance, actress Lainie Kazan approached him because she had misplaced a string of rosary beads that she needed for her next scene. He retrieved a set of rosary beads from an usherette's car just moments before the scene. (Courtesy of DT.)

JESUS CHRIST SUPERSTAR. Rock opera *Jesus Christ Superstar* first appeared at the Playhouse in 1971 and then again in 1974. Audiences were thrilled when Ted Neeley, who played Jesus in the 1971 motion picture version, joined the Wilmington cast in 1996 and 2006. For the past 40 years, Neeley has made a career of playing Jesus in stage productions. After the show and still very much in character, Neeley remained until late hours greeting his Wilmington fans. (Both, courtesy of HML.)

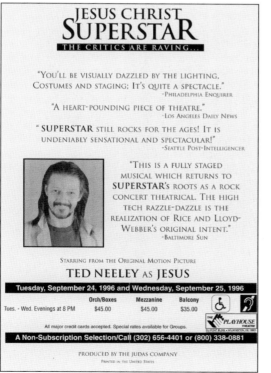

PAJAMA GAME. During a production of *Pajama Game*, DuPont Theatre staff invited patrons to attend the opening-night show in their pajamas. Theater usherettes joined in the fun, outfitted in luxurious white bathrobes provided by the Hotel du Pont. (Courtesy of Nancy McEwen.)

2010 BROADWAY PRODUCTIONS. From left to right, DuPont Theatre staff members Diana Milburn, Diana Hunt, Diane Angeline, and Bea Manley, along with theater manager John Gardner, pose with hard hats on stage to represent the theater's commitment to safety during each Broadway season. Production posters for 2010, including *A Chorus Line*, *Hairspray*, and *Xanadu* hang behind them. Posters not shown from the season are *Legally Blonde* and *Wizard of Oz*. (Photograph by Joe del Tufo.)

BLUE MAN GROUP. One of the messiest productions at the DuPont Theatre was the 2011 *Blue Man Group.* A trio of men painted blue entertained audiences with cereal, Twinkies, bananas, and other food products. Laundering their costumes had ruined so many washers and dryers at other theaters that the production company insisted on bringing its own equipment. (Courtesy of DT.)

CELEBRITY PETS. DuPont hospitality staff members posed with dog whisperer Cesar Millan and his trained pit bull, Junior, following his March 2011 appearance. Show pets are as much a part of the production as the actors. Theater employees have assisted in clipping the nails of performers' cats as well as walking their dogs. Lauren Bacall held her dog on her lap for the question and answer portion of her Smart Talk Series appearance. (Courtesy of DT.)

EXTERIOR MARQUEE. Here is a view of the Market Street DuPont Theatre entrance as it appeared in 2011. The extended red marquee that displays the DuPont oval has replaced the vertical sign that once said "Playhouse" in neon lights. DuPont Theatre banners in royal purple and gold hang, and 2011–2012 Broadway Series posters line the building. (Courtesy of DT.)

APPENDIX
CURTAIN CALL

The following is a list of just some of the famous names who have appeared on the DuPont Theatre stage over the past 100 seasons of entertainment.

Don Ameche
Julie Andrews
Louis Armstrong
Fred and Adele Astaire
Tallulah Bankhead
Ethel, John, and Lionel Barrymore
Ingrid Bergman
Marlon Brando
Jim Brickman
Billie Burke
George Carlin
Carol Channing
Kristin Chenoweth
Bette Davis
Patty Duke
Mia Farrow
Jane Fonda
Joan Fontaine
Whoopi Goldberg
Betty Grable
Joel Grey
George Hamilton
Goldie Hawn
Helen Hayes

Katharine Hepburn
Lena Horne
Al Jolson
Tom Jones
Nathan Lane
Michael Learned
Lorna Luft
Jayne Meadows
Ethel Merman
Cesar Millan
Ann Miller
Liza Minnelli
Rosie O'Donnell
Christopher Plummer
Robert Redford
Debbie Reynolds
Ginger Rogers
Mickey Rooney
Isabella Rossellini
Susan Stroman
Tommy Tune
Buddy Valastro
Orson Welles
Mae West

BIBLIOGRAPHY

"Auspicious Opening of the New Playhouse." *Wilmington Morning News*, October 16, 1913.

Crosland, Philip. *75th Anniversary, The Playhouse*. California: Sequoia Communications, Inc., 1987.

DuPont Building construction photographs, Accession 76.341, Hagley Museum and Library.

Hess, Maria. *Celebrating 90 Years at the Playhouse Theatre*. Wilmington, DE: The Playhouse Theatre, 2002.

Lynch, Kathleen (daughter of John A. Bader). Personal Files. 1913.

McNinch, Marjorie. *Wilmington in Vintage Postcards*. Charleston, SC: Arcadia Publishing, 2000.

Morgan, Donald. *History of the Wilmington Playhouse 1930–45*. Master's thesis, University of Delaware, 1964.

"Playhouse Gets National Praise." *Journal Every Evening*, September 27, 1952.

"Playhouse Marking 60th Anniversary." *Journal Every Evening*, October 10, 1973.

"Playhouse Marks Forty-Third 'Birth' Anniversary in April." *Journal Every Evening*, March 19, 1956.

"Playhouse Undergoes a Face-lift." *Wilmington Morning News*, July 25, 1976. Records of the DuPont Theatre, Accession 2150, Hagley Museum and Library.

Simmons, Joseph John. *History of the Wilmington Playhouse 1913–30*. Master's thesis, University of Delaware, 1963.

ABOUT DUPONT

DuPont (NYSE: DD) has been bringing world-class science and engineering to the global marketplace in the form of innovative products, materials, and services since 1802. The company believes that by collaborating with customers, governments, NGOs, and thought leaders, we can help find solutions to such global challenges as providing enough healthy food for people everywhere, decreasing dependence on fossil fuels, and protecting life and the environment. For additional information about DuPont and its commitment to inclusive innovation, please visit http://www.dupont.com.

DISCOVER THOUSANDS OF LOCAL HISTORY BOOKS
FEATURING MILLIONS OF VINTAGE IMAGES

Arcadia Publishing, the leading local history publisher in the United States, is committed to making history accessible and meaningful through publishing books that celebrate and preserve the heritage of America's people and places.

Find more books like this at
www.arcadiapublishing.com

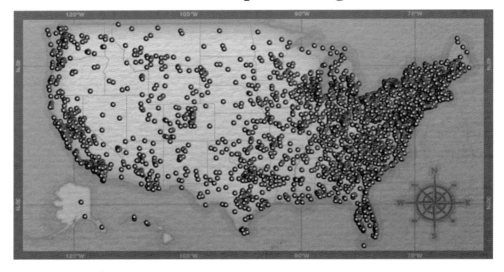

Search for your hometown history, your old stomping grounds, and even your favorite sports team.

Consistent with our mission to preserve history on a local level, this book was printed in South Carolina on American-made paper and manufactured entirely in the United States. Products carrying the accredited Forest Stewardship Council (FSC) label are printed on 100 percent FSC-certified paper.

MADE IN THE

USA